The Drug Abuse Prevention Library

Ritalin: Its Use and Abuse

Today, 2.5 million kids and adults in the United States have a prescription for Ritalin. Much of it ends up on the streets as a drug of abuse.

The Drug Abuse Prevention Library

Ritalin: Its Use and Abuse

Eileen Beal

The Rosen Publishing Group, Inc.
New York

This book could not have been written without the help of the wonderful information gods and goddesses at the Cleveland Heights/University Heights Library in Cleveland Heights, Ohio. I thank all the people who did reference and Internet searches, made calls, checked sources, confirmed name spellings and addresses, and were always ready—even at five minutes to nine PM—to go that extra step to get the facts.

Ritalin® is a registered trademark of Novartis Pharmaceuticals Corporation.

The people pictured in this book are only models. They in no way practice or endorse the activities illustrated. Captions serve only to explain the subjects of photographs and do not in any way imply a connection between the real-life models and the staged situations.

Published in 1999, 2003 by The Rosen Publishing Group, Inc.
29 East 21st Street, New York, NY 10010

Revised Edition 2003

Library of Congress Cataloging-in-Publication Data
Beal, Eileen.
    Ritalin : its use and abuse / Eileen Beal.
        p. cm. — (The drug abuse prevention library)
    Includes bibliographical references and index.
    Summary: Describes the medical uses of the prescription drug Ritalin, the problems presented by overprescribing it, its potential for abuse, and ways to prevent such abuse.
        ISBN 0-8239-3759-3 (lib. bdg.)
        1. Methylphenidate hydrochloride. 2. Attention-deficit hyperactivity disorder—Chemotherapy. 3. Teenagers—Drug use. 4. Children—Drug use. [1. Methylphenidate hydrochloride. 2. Attention-deficit hyperactivity disorder. 3. Drugs.] I. Title. II. Series.
RJ506.H9B43 1999
616.85'89061—dc21   98-27089

Manufactured in the United States of America

Contents

Introduction

"*I was twelve years old when I was diagnosed with attention deficit hyperactivity disorder [ADHD],*" says Miranda, now sixteen. "*My doctor suggested I try a drug called Ritalin. I worried, though, that if I took Ritalin everyone would think I was some kind of delinquent who needed drugs to stay in control. But after talking with my parents, I decided to try Ritalin, at least for a short time.*

"*I wouldn't call Ritalin a miracle drug. But in combination with therapy, it sure has helped me deal with problems such as paying attention, getting assignments done on time, and getting along with people at school and at home.*"

Doctors are prescribing Ritalin to more children and teenagers than ever. Today 2.5 million children and adults in the United States alone have prescriptions for Ritalin.

However, the decision to take Ritalin is not an easy one. Ritalin may cause uncomfortable side effects in some people. Those taking the drug may also feel embarrassed, ashamed, or angry that they need it. Even worse, they may become targets for people who want to abuse the drug.

As a result, teenagers with attention deficit disorder (ADD) or ADHD may feel pressure from their classmates, friends, or even family members to sell, share, or give away their medication. This pressure can be very hard to resist.

This book will tell you about Ritalin—what it is and how it developed. If you have ADD or ADHD, it will also help you decide if you should take Ritalin to treat your disorder. Finally, it will give you some tips on how to deal with the pressure to share your medication. You can learn to avoid the people and places that will put you at risk for peer pressure. You can also learn to say no to someone who wants your Ritalin.

If you have ADD or ADHD, you may find it difficult to concentrate in class or remain focused on your schoolwork.

What Is Ritalin?

Newspaper headlines, national reports, magazine articles, and TV and radio shows have made Ritalin a major topic of discussion and debate. So what exactly is Ritalin?

A PRESCRIPTION DRUG

Ritalin is the brand name for the prescription drug methylphenidate, (meh-thal-FEH-na-dayt). Methylphenidate is a generic drug produced by several companies. Though generic drugs and brand-name drugs are similar in their chemical makeup and effectiveness, generic drugs usually cost less. Ritalin and other brands of methylphenidate are used to help treat two closely related medical disorders—attention deficit disorder and attention deficit hyperactivity disorder. Dexedrine and Cylert are two other types of drugs that are also used to treat ADD and ADHD.

Although ADD and ADHD are often grouped together, they have slightly different symptoms. People with ADD tend to be inattentive, unfocused, and easily distracted. People with ADHD have the same symptoms as those with ADD, but they are impulsive or hyperactive as well. These two disorders are fairly common, especially in young people. The majority of sufferers are boys, but many girls also have one of these medical disorders.

Scientists think that ADD and ADHD occur because certain chemicals in the brain are missing. Because of the chemical problem, the brain is unable to properly use chemicals called neurotransmitters, which carry nerve impulses through the brain. Ritalin does not cure ADD or ADHD, but it does improve a person's ability to be calm and to concentrate. Then it is easier to work on other problems associated with ADD and ADHD, such as poor social skills, low grades, family problems, depression, and low self-esteem.

Some people also worry that doctors are prescribing Ritalin to young people who do not really need medication. In addition, experts are concerned about Ritalin's potential for abuse. Dozens of books and hundreds of articles have been written about the pros and cons of Ritalin use—and its growing abuse.

WHERE DOES RITALIN COME FROM?

Ritalin is not found in nature. It is a synthetic drug, created by chemists in a laboratory. All the Ritalin produced in the United States is made by one company, Novartis Pharmaceuticals Corporation. Methylphenidate, in generic form, is produced by several companies. These companies use a formula very similar to Ritalin.

CLASS II STIMULANT

According to the U.S. Drug Enforcement Administration (DEA), methylphenidate is a Class II stimulant drug. The DEA ranks drugs and medications on a scale from I to IV. Ritalin's ranking as a Class II drug means that it is a controlled substance—legally available only with a prescription from a doctor. It also means that, while it has a high level of usefulness as a prescription medication, Ritalin also poses a risk for abuse as an illegal stimulant. A stimulant is a drug, such as an amphetamine, that increases the body's heart and breathing rates. A stimulant may give you a buzz or make you feel high. It may make you excited, happy, and energetic, or it may make you agitated, anxious, and irritable.

Ritalin's illegal use can lead to addiction. If it is not used wisely, it can be extremely dangerous. That's one of the reasons that the U.S. government puts it in the same class of drugs as cocaine, morphine, and opium.

It is important to remember that people with ADD or ADHD cannot become addicted to Ritalin. You will find out why later in this book. Therefore, information about Ritalin abuse and addiction pertains only to people who do not suffer from one of these disorders.

Chapter 2

The Pros and Cons of Taking Ritalin

"*It was hard for me to make friends,*" confesses fifteen-year-old John. "*Other kids thought I came on too strong. Also, I was always getting in trouble with teachers for not paying attention in class. I was kept back twice due to failing grades. I never thought Ritalin would make such a difference, but it helped me concentrate better and work without getting distracted. My grades improved a lot and I became more laid back. For the first time, I could say I had a social life.*"

RITALIN'S POSITIVE AND NEGATIVE ASPECTS

Ritalin and generic, or nonbrand, forms of methylphenidate are stimulants. Stimulants are chemicals that affect the brain by increasing alertness, attention, and energy.

13

Some teens use Ritalin or other stimulants to help them through all-night study sessions. However, when the stimulant wears off, a person feels burned-out and exhausted.

Many people who take Ritalin experience a boost in energy, or a "high," that can last anywhere from a few minutes to several hours. After the high wears off, however, they often feel sick, depressed, and exhausted. Some stimulants, such as cocaine and amphetamines, often leave the abuser wanting more of the drug. This strong desire to have more of a drug is known as addiction.

In people with ADD or ADHD, however, Ritalin works in the opposite way. It filters out distractions and allows people with these ailments to concentrate on a specific activity.

This is hard for people with ADD and ADHD because they are constantly bombarded by many different impulses at one time. The impulses can become so overwhelming that people suffering from them can't process information or control their reactions. When used properly, Ritalin can help people suffering from these ailments become more focused and live more normal lives.

A SURGE IN RITALIN USE

An estimated 70 percent of people diagnosed with ADD and ADHD use Ritalin to help them deal with their symptoms. This makes Ritalin the most commonly used stimulant in the treatment of these diseases.

Steven Hyman, M.D., director of the National Institute of Mental Health (NIMH), says Ritalin has been "highly effective in treating all the signs" of ADD and ADHD. Over 160 studies have shown that Ritalin improves the lives of "at least 80 percent" of kids with ADD and ADHD.

However, Hyman also warns that Ritalin is being prescribed much too often, and even in cases where it is unnecessary. Many doctors, child psychologists, and family therapists agree. According to the World

Health Organization's International Narcotics Control Board (INCB), Americans consume 90 percent of the world's Ritalin supply and are taking the drug more than ever before. It is estimated that over four million children currently take the drug.

From these statistics, it is not surprising that many medical professionals believe that Ritalin is being prescribed for kids who may not need the medication at all. Busy parents might think that medicating a child who acts up is an easy way of solving their problems.

Dr. Stephan Evans, associate professor of psychology at James Madison University, says, "Many health-care providers are often too quick to diagnose ADHD after even a short ten-minute office visit with a pediatrician, and medications are also too quickly relied upon as a first line of treatment because they are safe and easy to use."

Doctors must understand that not all behavior problems are cured with medication. Many problems result from conflicts at school or at home. Prescribing Ritalin is often a quick fix that masks symptoms, but does nothing to solve the real problems the child may be facing. Often, only discussion and therapy can deal with these deeper emotional issues.

"I always get really stressed out during final exams," confesses thirteen-year-old Hana. "So a friend gave me some blue pills called Ritalin. He said if I took them I would ace my exams.

"Then one night, when I was too tired to study, I took a pill. I was flying high almost right away. I couldn't sit still. When I finally lay down to bed, I couldn't sleep. By the time of my exam, I was exhausted. The Ritalin had worn off and left me burnt-out. It also gave me a terrible headache. Needless to say, I completely flunked the exam."

RITALIN ON THE RISE

Ritalin works to calm people with ADD and ADHD. In people who don't have either of these disorders, however, it produces a high similar to that produced by stimulants such as cocaine. In many American classrooms today, it is common to find that 25 percent of kids have been prescribed Ritalin or its generic equivalent. As a result, it is extremely easy for kids who want to abuse Ritalin to get their hands on the drug. On the street, Ritalin is known as the "chill pill," "Vitamin R," "the R Ball," and "kiddie cocaine."

Ritalin is very dangerous when abused, especially when mixed with alcohol.

According to *Monitoring the Future*, a yearly survey of legal and illegal drug use published by the University of Michigan, Ritalin abuse is rising, especially in suburban middle schools and high schools and in colleges. Some people use it because it keeps them awake and focused. Others use it because it gets them high. Still others use it as a diet aid since one side effect is that it decreases appetite.

For people who don't have ADD or ADHD however, taking Ritalin can create many dangerous health risks. Insomnia, increased heart rate, high blood pressure, hyperthermia (extremely high body temperature), nausea and vomiting, digestive problems, abdominal pain, dizziness, headaches, convulsions, seizures, feelings of anxiety, paranoia, and aggressive behavior are all side effects of unneeded Ritalin.

While death due to nonmedical Ritalin use is uncommon, it has been known to occur. There is no safe way to experiment with nonmedical Ritalin.

Should I Take Ritalin?

As a prescription medication, Ritalin has been around for a long time. It was patented in 1950, but had been around for several decades before then. Back then, doctors used Ritalin to treat adults for narcolepsy, a sleep disorder. In 1937, scientists discovered that it could also be used to treat children with severely disruptive behavior and hyperactivity problems. Since the early 1960s, Ritalin has been used to treat ADD and ADHD. It has been the most commonly prescribed drug for these disorders since the early 1980s.

Because Ritalin can help people with ADD and ADHD calm down, focus their attention, and concentrate on projects and tasks, it can improve performance at school. Children and teenagers who use Ritalin to treat their ADD or ADHD may find that their grades

Ritalin can improve concentration in people with ADD and ADHD. An improved ability to focus and pay attention can make participating in activities easier and more fun.

improve. They may want to participate in more extracurricular activities, such as sports teams, clubs, and the school band. They also may have fewer disciplinary problems when on Ritalin.

Ritalin can also improve social and interpersonal skills. As a result, it can make life at home easier, too. People on Ritalin often argue and fight with family and friends less frequently. They often feel less tension and communicate more effectively with the people around them.

Finally, Ritalin can decrease the forgetfulness and inappropriate, spontaneous behaviors that ADD and ADHD often cause. These difficulties, which can include everything from fidgeting to foul language to fighting, can harm a person's relationships with others and destroy his or her social life. A person on Ritalin may find that day-to-day life becomes much happier. However, despite all these advantages, the decision to take Ritalin is often difficult for people with ADD or ADHD.

Linda was thirteen when she discovered she had ADHD. Though she was relieved there was a medical explanation for her condition, she didn't want to have to take the Ritalin her doctor prescribed.

"I didn't want people at school to know I had a mental disorder because I took the drug," she remembers. "Also, I had heard all this bad stuff about Ritalin in the news.

"Finally, with the help of a therapist, I worked out my fears and problems about ADHD and taking drugs. I now take Ritalin regularly and it's become a daily part of my life. I'm not ashamed that I need medication because it's helped me a lot."

MAKING A DIFFICULT DECISION

If you decide to take Ritalin or a generic form of methylphenidate for your ADD or ADHD, you are doing much more than simply taking your "meds," or your medication. You are taking control of your disorder, your life, and your future.

To ensure that you make the right decision, talk with your parents and family physician. You may also want the advice of a school counselor, psychologist, minister, or rabbi. You may want to confide in a teacher, scout leader, or another adult you trust. And, almost always, you will want to talk with your friends.

According to Lynn Weiss, Ph.D., author of *Give Your ADD Teen a Chance*, the following are questions you will want to ask yourself or your doctor:

✔ **What options do I have?**

✔ **What does the medication do?**

✔ **What are the side effects?**

✔ **What will I feel like when I'm on the medication?**

✔ How will it change me?

✔ When should I call my doctor with a question?

✔ How long will it take to work?

✔ What if it doesn't work?

✔ How should I take Ritalin?

✔ What should I do if the other kids make fun of me?

✔ When can I stop taking Ritalin if I want to?

✔ Can I become addicted to Ritalin?

✔ Can I use it when I need to study a lot and then not use it at other times?

✔ Should I talk to someone who takes Ritalin?

There are many ways to manage your ADD or ADHD. If you decide to take medication, you and your doctor will work out a dosage and schedule that is right for you.

CHOOSING A SCHEDULE THAT WORKS

If you are taking medication for ADD or ADHD, it's up to you and your doctor to find the right medication, dosage, and schedule. Different methods work for different people. Some people take Ritalin, others take a generic form of methylphenidate. Some take long-acting pills, others take short-acting ones. Some take their prescription pills twice a day, others take them three times a day. Some take their pills every day, others take them only when they have a specific task to do, skipping them on weekends, during vacations, and in the summertime.

"I had just started junior high when I began using Ritalin," says Pedro, fifteen. *"I thought it would be tough to fit in if everyone knew that I had ADD. When my doctor told me about long-acting pills, I thought they would be the perfect solution. The problem was that they contained such a high dosage of Ritalin that they knocked me out.*

"So I tried taking short-acting pills with a lower dosage of Ritalin. This time, the results were great. Even though this meant taking a pill at school, it ended up not being such a big deal. I just stopped by the nurse's office on the way to lunch everyday and it became so routine that after a week or so nobody even cared."

BALANCING THE PROS AND CONS

If you and your doctor decide to treat your ADD or ADHD with Ritalin, you have to weigh the medication's pros and cons. There are many of each.

The pros often include: easy-to-take form; increased ability to concentrate and focus attention; less overall restlessness and hyperactivity; less impulsive behavior; less aggressive behavior; improved grades in school; and improved social life.

The cons often include: loss of appetite and weight loss; inability to sleep, usually due to a "booster" pill taken in the afternoon; stomach pain; headaches; dizziness; dry mouth; and constipation. Some people also experience blurred vision, mood swings, depression, and tics (voice or facial spasms).

For a very small number of people, Ritalin can cause life-threatening side effects. These include hypertension, a racing heart, and possibly a rare form of liver cancer. If combined with alcohol, Ritalin can be extremely dangerous and even life-threatening. Ritalin doesn't work in treating ADD or ADHD in people who suffer from certain other disorders. Be sure to consult your doctor if you are experiencing any side effects while on Ritalin.

Finally, do not expect Ritalin to cure all of your problems. ADD and ADHD are complex disorders that can cause many types of social and emotional difficulties. Ritalin can help control your symptoms, but you may still want to consider other forms of treatment.

You can attend therapy to deal with your emotions. You can also get training in areas such as study skills, organizational methods, and time management. Often, these methods, combined with medication, are the best form of treatment.

Chapter 4

Is Ritalin Addictive?

"My family is really into natural medicines," says Ida, thirteen. "We don't even have aspirin in the house. So when I was finally diagnosed with ADD and the doctor suggested Ritalin, we all resisted. The problem was that no natural remedy we tried helped me.

"My parents and I worried that because it was a stimulant, Ritalin would be addictive. But the doctor promised us that people with ADD couldn't become addicted to Ritalin. He also promised that it would work. He was right."

FEAR OF ADDICTION

As you learned earlier, Ritalin is a Class II stimulant—a prescription drug with a great potential for abuse. Many teens fear that they may become addicted to Ritalin.

Work out a regular schedule for taking your Ritalin. When you do so, it's easier to remember to take your pills.

However, when used as prescribed, Ritalin has been found to be a very safe medication for people with ADD and ADHD. Current studies and years of successful use suggest that people who have ADD or ADHD cannot abuse Ritalin. This is because:

- **The tablets are taken under the supervision of a responsible adult, such as a parent, teacher, guidance counselor, or school nurse.**

- Ritalin replaces a chemical that is missing in the brains of people who have ADD or ADHD. These people do not become overstimulated or high on their prescription dose of Ritalin. Instead, exactly the opposite happens. Ritalin calms them and helps them to focus and concentrate.

- People with ADD and ADHD do not need increasing doses of Ritalin to maintain its medical benefits, and they do not develop a craving for it.

- Finally, teens often stop taking Ritalin as they mature. The symptoms of ADD and ADHD, such as impulsivity, poor concentration, and a short attention span, create many academic, social, emotional, and work-related challenges. However, many people learn other ways to cope with these difficulties and no longer need medication.

MOVING BEYOND RITALIN

Ultimately, in consultation with parents and doctors, many teens decide that they do not need Ritalin anymore. If you are on Ritalin and decide to stop taking it, you don't go through the withdrawal symptoms that affect someone addicted to other types of drugs.

When a person is addicted to a drug, he or she can experience painful withdrawal symptoms when he or she does not have it. Symptoms can include chills, sweating, convulsions, and nausea. However, according to Thomas W. Phelan, Ph.D., a clinical psychologist, a person with ADD or ADHD will not experience drug withdrawal because he or she is not dependent upon Ritalin in the way that someone who is addicted would be.

"How it happens, we are not sure," admits Phelan, author of *All About Attention Deficit Disorder*, "but whatever the case, some people can stop the meds and still continue to function well." So it is important to remember that, if you begin to take Ritalin, you may not have to take it forever. If you feel you may be ready to stop, you can do so fairly easily. Before doing so, however, be sure to consult with your doctor and parents and get their approval.

Chapter 5

Ritalin Abuse

"*I*'m so lucky that my two best friends have Ritalin prescriptions that they share with me," says Joe, sixteen. "*Before I started using Ritalin, I had a major body image problem. I hated my weight, but I couldn't lose it because I loved to eat. Now when I take Ritalin I barely ever feel hungry. I feel happier, too. I don't know what I'd do without my two best friends. I'd have to start buying Ritalin on the street.*"

RISING IN POPULARITY

The above is an example of Ritalin abuse. As we saw before, there was a great increase in the 1990s in Ritalin being prescribed for young people with ADD, ADHD, and other behavioral problems. At the same time, Ritalin's popularity as a recreational drug for teens soared. This is hardly surprising when

People may plead with you or bully you for your medication. It's hard to say no, but remember, you need it yourself to manage your ADD or ADHD.

one considers that in some American schools close to a quarter of all high-school seniors have prescriptions for Ritalin.

Ritalin is so easy to obtain that many abusers don't even need to pay up to $20 per pill, the price that tablets can sell for on the street. They can simply get other kids to share their legally prescribed pills.

Brad's ten-year-old sister, Dee, takes Ritalin for her ADHD. Brad's dad gives Dee three tablets a day. Although he keeps the bottle locked in the medicine cabinet, Brad made a copy of the key. Brad worked out that one Ritalin tablet *costs his dad about 30 cents. But he can get $10 a pill when he sells the Ritalin.*

It's not as if Brad's a dealer. He only sells to kids he knows at school. And he only takes Dee's Ritalin when her prescription has been renewed and the bottle is full of pills. His dad never even notices the difference.

So far, Brad has made enough money to buy a lot of cool new clothes. He wears them to all the parties he is suddenly being invited to, parties where Ritalin is taken by many of the kids.

THE RISKS OF SHARING

The majority of Ritalin abuse involves people with legal prescriptions for the drug. Sharing Ritalin can lead to problems for everyone. An insufficient amount of pills often interferes with the prescription of the person who needs the drug. And casually taking prescription drugs can be very harmful for someone who doesn't need them.

Lani found out that her new friend Roberto was taking Ritalin for his ADD.

"Rob, if only I had known. Can you give me a couple of pills for Rachel's party tomorrow? Of course you're welcome to come, too."

Your friends may pressure you to share your Ritalin, but doing so will put you and the people you share with at risk.

Roberto wanted to go to Rachel's party, so he gave Lani the pills. But after the party, Lani kept asking him for more and more. Two weeks later, Roberto was almost out of pills. Worried his parents would notice the decrease, he stopped taking his medication. Almost immediately, studying became a big effort and he flunked two important exams.

A SERIOUS CRIME

Under federal and state laws, possessing Ritalin without a prescription is a felony. Both the person who shares or sells it and the person who uses or buys it are breaking the law. Depending on the amount of the drug, the ages of the people involved, and the location of the transaction, dealing Ritalin could mean a prison term of up to forty-five years and a fine of up to $10,000.

METHODS OF RITALIN CONSUMPTION

There are several popular ways Ritalin abusers consume the drug in order for it to have a stronger effect. They may take a whole or a half tablet. They can also crush the pills into powder, which they snort through the nose. They can also mix the crushed pills with liquid and inject the mixture into the bloodstream with a needle. Each of these methods of consumption can have hazardous side effects for the user.

Snorting Ritalin can produce severe headaches, nosebleeds, permanent damage to the lining of the nose, seizures, and even strokes. Injecting it can cause blood clots, problems with blood circulation, blood poisoning, hepatitis, and even AIDS. Furthermore, many experts believe that Ritalin is a "gateway" drug, or a drug that leads to the abuse of stronger and more dangerous drugs such as heroin and cocaine.

PHYSICAL AND PSYCHOLOGICAL ADDICTION

There are two ways someone can become addicted to Ritalin: physically and psychologically. When your body craves a drug so badly that it can't function without it, you are physically addicted. In fact, when addicts can't get their hands on the drug they are addicted to, their bodies may suffer from withdrawal. Withdrawal symptoms can include shaking, sweating, mood swings, nightmares, and hallucinations.

Some Ritalin addicts have also been known to experience "formication," hallucinations that make them believe that bugs are crawling under their skin.

People who suffer from psychological addiction take a drug because of a mental or emotional need. Often, the addict continues taking the drug for fear of experiencing the withdrawal symptoms mentioned above. People who are physically and psychologically addicted to a drug have been known to stop at nothing to get more of it.

While there is no proof that Ritalin causes physical addiction, numerous studies have shown that Ritalin is psychologically addictive. Many teens who abuse Ritalin admit to being psychologically addicted to the drug. They believe that if they don't take Ritalin, it will be harder for them to study, or that they will be less confident or entertaining. Once you think you need Ritalin in order to function, you are on your way to becoming addicted to it.

THE ROAD TO ADDICTION

Becoming addicted to Ritalin is not as hard as you might think. In general, addiction is a four-step process.

1. Experimentation. The first time you use a drug is like an experiment. You want to see how the drug will affect you. If Ritalin makes you feel good the first time you take it, chances are you will want to take it again.

2. Abuse. As you take more Ritalin, you will need to take larger amounts and take it more frequently in order to feel the same high.

3. Dependency. You can no longer control how much Ritalin you use, or how often you use it.

4. Addiction. You need Ritalin to get through everyday tasks. It becomes more important than anything else.

SIGNS OF ADDICTION

Anyone can become addicted to Ritalin. People of all ages, races, and backgrounds are equally at risk. A person can be considered an addict if he or she:

- Gets high on Ritalin on a regular basis

- Lies about taking Ritalin, the amount taken, and how often he or she takes it

- Uses Ritalin when alone

- Believes it's impossible to have fun, relax, or do well in school without taking Ritalin

- Takes risks, such as driving while high

- Acts aggressively or violently

- Begins to experience problems with his or her performance at school or work and with his or her relationships at home and with peers

- Makes promises to stop using Ritalin, but can't keep them

Chapter 6

Making Ritalin a Part of Your Life

" *At first I did everything I could to hide the fact that I have ADD and needed to take Ritalin,"* confesses Marly, thirteen. *"But it got to the point where I was sneaking down to the nurse's office so no one would find out. Of course, I couldn't keep this a secret for long.*

"It's a pain that people know I need to take the drug. Some kids ask me to share my Ritalin, and when I don't they get mad and call me a junkie. I really wish I didn't have to take Ritalin, but it has made my life easier in so many other ways."

RITALIN'S REPUTATION

The media blizzard of information on ADD, ADHD, and Ritalin often doesn't talk about the psychological, personal, and emotional

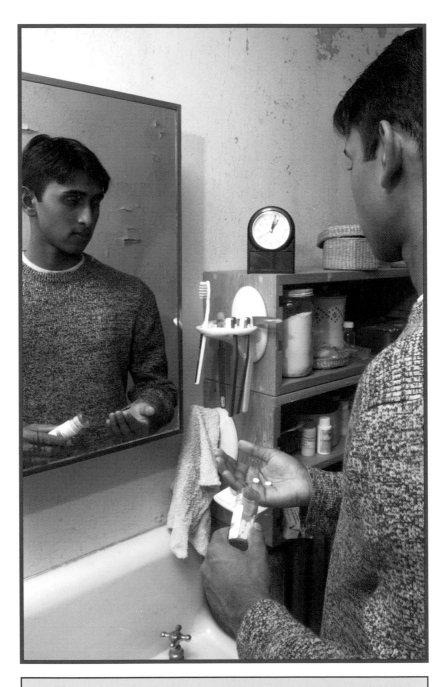

There are many ways to manage your ADD and ADHD. Medication is one of the most common. Other methods include learning study and organizational skills and time management techniques.

problems that accompany a prescription for Ritalin. Many people think they know what kind of problems people with ADD or ADHD have—they are out of control and have to take pills to get their act together.

This hasty diagnosis causes anger, bitterness, confusion, embarrassment, and shame for people who take Ritalin. People with ADD or ADHD know they need Ritalin to help them manage their disorder. However, the media attention to and publicity about ADD, ADHD, and Ritalin place a stigma—a feeling of personal shame—on people with ADD or ADHD. This stigma also makes going to a parent, nurse, or teacher to receive medicine a daily ordeal.

When classmates and friends know you are taking Ritalin, they may make comments about "crazy pills," "chill pills," and "spaz drugs." They may call you names, too. Worst of all, they may subtly, or even obviously, pressure you to share your medication with them. You may not know what to do.

ADD AND ADHD ARE MEDICAL DISORDERS

The stigma attached to ADD and ADHD (and needing to use a drug to manage them) also means that many teens often get less support from family and friends. Others often see ADD and ADHD as laziness or as behavioral instead of biological problems. They often think it can be cured with a better attitude, harder work, or more self-discipline. They may not understand that, for someone with ADD or ADHD, Ritalin can be a necessity.

Many teens do manage their ADD or ADHD without medication. They may go to therapy to learn to cope with their anger and frustration. They may also learn study and organizational skills and practice time management techniques. There are many ways to learn to cope with ADD and ADHD.

However, these people's successes strengthen the false belief that if the person with ADD or ADHD would just try harder he or she would not need Ritalin. The teens who do not need Ritalin, however, usually have only mild or very moderate ADD or ADHD symptoms. Teens with more serious disorders may not be able to function nearly as well without Ritalin.

Media hype and a lack of support from family and friends can damage the feelings of pride, self-esteem, and self-worth of a person with ADD or ADHD. He or she may wonder, "Since I need a pill to be more in control, more social, and more accepted, what kind of person am I?"

ADD and ADHD are medical problems, like nearsightedness or diabetes. They are not under your control. You are born with them. Like many medical disorders, ADD and ADHD can be treated with medication. Ritalin cannot cure these disorders, but it will help you live with them. By choosing to take Ritalin, you are not admitting you are helpless and out of control. Instead, you are taking control. You are trying to solve your problems and manage your medical disorder.

"My whole family had a tough time dealing with my ADHD before it was diagnosed," remembers sixteen-year-old Rayid. *"My parents had read a lot about how wonderful Ritalin was. They thought it would solve all our problems.*

"Ritalin helped me concentrate, but I didn't become a genius overnight, like my parents expected I would. They were disappointed when I didn't get straight A's and when my teachers said I still had attention problems. I wondered if something else was wrong with me.

"So I went to a psychologist and learned that the problem wasn't the Ritalin—it was me. Ritalin could help control my symptoms, but the rest, like changing my study habits and getting organized, was up to me to take care of. I learned that for as helpful Ritalin is, it's not a cure-all drug."

RITALIN IS NOT A CRUTCH

If you take Ritalin for ADD or ADHD, you can neither get high from it nor become addicted. However, you can still abuse it. You can do this by using Ritalin as an academic, social, or emotional crutch. Using something as a crutch means that you blame it for your problems, mistakes, and failures. You use it as an excuse for everything that goes wrong. If you have a crutch, you do not need to try to improve or work harder because you can tell yourself and others that there's simply nothing you can do. You can pretend that none of your difficulties are really your fault.

ADD and ADHD can cause many problems in your life beyond agitation and hyperactivity. People with these disorders often have poor study habits, lack of social skills, loss of self-esteem and self-worth, and frustration and anger. Ritalin is not a cure for these difficulties. You cannot expect it to solve all the problems in your life. It won't necessarily make you a smarter, happier, more popular, and more successful person overnight.

However, Ritalin can help you to control your ADD or ADHD. Ritalin is not a cure for ADD or ADHD, but it can be a key to acquiring more effective study habits, better social skills, and greater self-esteem and self-worth.

PEER PRESSURE

If you take Ritalin for ADD or ADHD, you may often have to deal with peer pressure. Peer pressure is when your friends or your peers try to push you to do something you are not sure you want to do.

Everyone feels peer pressure. Everyone wants to fit in, be accepted, and be important. These feelings are normal and natural. But some people try to take advantage of other people's need for approval by convincing them to do things that are bad for them. If you are taking Ritalin, you may be pressured to share your pills.

If you share your medication, you will lose the tool you need to succeed in school, at

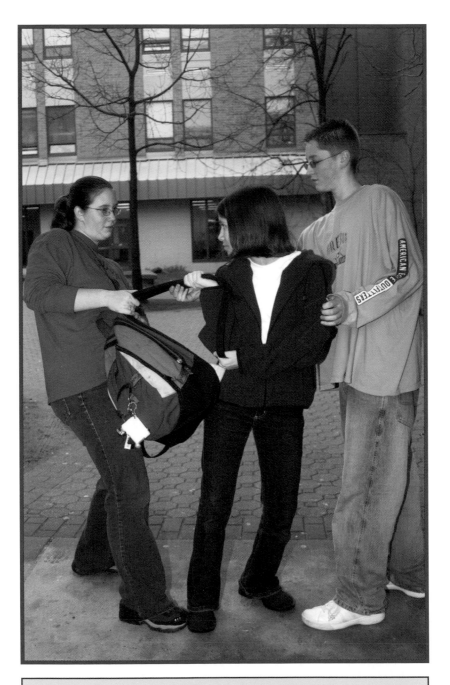

People may ask, beg, or bully you for your Ritalin. Being ready for such situations will help you say no when they occur.

home, and in social situations. If you do not share, your so-called friends may accuse you of being stingy, selfish, nerdy, and self-centered. Also, some people even experience physical pressure to hand over their pills. School and neighborhood bullies have threatened and beaten up people for their medication. In addition, sometimes family members, even parents, ask for, borrow, or steal their children's Ritalin. They either sell it or use it themselves.

You may agree that you should not share your medication with anyone, no matter what the circumstances. However, finding a way to refuse can be hard. You may know that you should refuse, but you probably need some advice on how to do it.

"I was really excited when Joann invited me to her party. We had never really been friends. And since I had been taking Ritalin for my ADHD, I had been feeling a lot more comfortable in social situations.

"I thought Joann was responding to the new me and that made me feel good. But then the day of her party, she called me up to ask if I could bring some of my 'chill pills' to the party. I then understood her sudden interest in me."

Chapter 7

Knowing How to Say No

"*I* guess because I've been taking Ritalin for four years, I forget that it's an addictive drug that can have dangerous side effects," says Alan, sixteen. "I used to share my Ritalin with my best friend, Jake. I never thought twice when he kept asking for more.

"Then one day Jake's mom called my mom in a panic from the hospital. She had found Jake in the living room after a party. He was lying on the floor having a seizure. After he had his stomach pumped, the doctors found traces of alcohol and Ritalin in his blood. Jake's mom wondered what I knew about the Ritalin and how Jake had become addicted to it.

"My Ritalin has always helped me. But it could have caused my best friend's death."

"For many teens," says Officer Daniel Howard of the Los Angeles Police Department, "it's only when something serious happens—they are arrested, someone is hurt, someone dies—that they get the wake-up call they need to think about the dangers of abusing Ritalin." But he also says that when that happens, teens usually do not know how to say no to sharing or dealing.

"It's not easy," admits Howard, "but there's a lot kids can do to deal with the situation . . . [or to] prevent the situation from coming up in the first place." There probably will be requests, pressures, and demands for your Ritalin, and you have to be ready.

GET THE FACTS

Educate Yourself About ADD or ADHD

Knowledge is power. You need to know about your medical disorder and the role Ritalin plays in helping you manage it. This will help you better explain why you cannot spare or share your medication.

Educate Yourself About Ritalin

"If you share or sell your medication," explains Howard, "you are breaking the law.

You and the person you give it to can be charged criminally for providing or abusing it.

"If it is exchanged on or near school property," he adds, "the legal penalties are even higher than if it's a 'street' transaction."

EDUCATE YOUR FRIENDS ABOUT RITALIN

Many of the people who ask you to share your Ritalin may think it gives you a high, too. They may think you are being selfish by keeping it for yourself. Explain that Ritalin is a medical necessity for you. Explain that it doesn't give you a high. Explain that when you do not take Ritalin (or when you take only half a pill) your ADD or ADHD becomes a problem. And keep explaining until your friends really hear what you are saying.

DON'T ANNOUNCE YOUR USE

There is nothing shameful about taking Ritalin. However, if people know that you take it, they may ask or pressure you to share it.

NEVER CARRY YOUR RITALIN WITH YOU

At school, on an outing, at camp, and in other public places, leave your pills with a teacher, nurse, or another adult you trust. Never leave

Taking your medication in an open place puts you at risk for peer pressure. Instead, leave your pills with a responsible adult and take them in private.

your medication in your backpack or locker, where it can be stolen.

Take Sustained-Release (SR) Pills

Sustained-release pills are a long-lasting form of Ritalin. These pills decrease the number of doses of Ritalin you must take each day. Their effect can last up to seven hours. If you take SR Ritalin, you will not have to go to the nurse's or principal's office to get your pills each day.

SR Ritalin may not work for everyone, however. Each person with ADD or ADHD responds differently to Ritalin and the other forms of methylphenidate. Some people simply cannot take the long-acting form of the pill. You can ask your doctor if it will work for you.

STAY OUT OF HARM'S WAY

Avoid people who may want to use, borrow, or steal your medication. The best way to deal with peer pressure is to stay away from the people who are pressuring you.

POWER UP MENTALLY

PSYCH YOURSELF UP TO SAY NO

Do what ace athletes and award-winning movie stars do when they are gearing up for stressful situations: use mental imaging. Paint a picture in your mind of how you will successfully say no when someone asks or pressures you for your pills.

For example, imagine being at school when a friend asks you to share your Ritalin with him or her for an all-night study session. Create a mental picture of yourself—complete with gestures, eye contact, and so forth—explaining how you need all the pills you are prescribed. Picture yourself telling him or her that you cannot share pills, not even with a friend.

Or imagine yourself explaining to the school thug who demands your medication that you do not carry your Ritalin with you. Picture yourself telling him or her that you are required to swallow each pill in front of the principal or school nurse.

Mental imaging works for two reasons: It helps you sort out feelings, fears, and frustrations and gets you emotionally and psychologically ready for real situations.

TALK ABOUT THE PRESSURES YOU ARE UNDER

"You need to talk about it when someone is asking you for your medication," explains Officer Howard. "It helps you get your feelings out in the open—the frustration you feel about having to use a medication, the fear of losing a friend, the anger when someone who is supposed to be a friend just wants to use you."

You can talk to many different people. At home, speak with your parents or other relatives you trust. At school, the school nurse, your guidance counselor, a teacher, or a

coach can help you. Scout leaders, minis-
ters, rabbis, and police officers are also
good sources of assistance. So are the
people staffing the phones at the local
health department or drug hotline. "You
don't have to talk face-to-face," Howard
stresses. "Make an anonymous call. Ask
questions. Get advice."

CALL IN REINFORCEMENTS

GET HELP WHEN YOU NEED IT

"If you are being pressured or threatened [for
your Ritalin], get help. You cannot fight that
kind of battle by yourself," says Howard. If
you feel as though someone might really hurt
you, tell someone immediately. Do not be
ashamed or embarrassed to ask for help.
Important things, such as your health and
well-being, are at stake.

JOIN A PEER SUPPORT GROUP

Many support groups exist for teens with ADD
and ADHD. These groups often discuss the
growing abuse of Ritalin and the increasing
pressures teens who take Ritalin are under to
share their medication. They will help you

share your feelings and frustrations, ask questions, and get advice. "In a peer group," explains Howard, "you learn from others' mistakes . . . and from their successes."

If you are currently taking Ritalin, or even just thinking about taking it, you are not alone. Many teens with ADD or ADHD are using Ritalin to help manage their disorders. For you, Ritalin may be a necessary medication. For others, it may be a recreational drug. Although other people may pressure you to share your Ritalin with them, you can refuse. Many people and organizations are willing to help you do just that. Using your Ritalin properly, in the way and for the reason it is prescribed, is the first step toward building a successful future. The choice is up to you.

Glossary

addiction The need to use drugs or alcohol compulsively and not be able to function without them.

anxiety A feeling of stress and uncertainty.

convulsion An uncontrollable muscle contraction that causes the body to shake.

dosage The amount of medication a doctor prescribes and the way he or she instructs you to take it.

drug abuse To use drugs or alcohol in a way that harms you and/or others.

generic drug A drug similar in chemical makeup and effectiveness to a brand-name drug, but which is often less expensive.

medication A drug taken to relieve pain, cure disease, or treat a disorder.

methylphenidate A generic prescription drug used to treat attention deficit disorder (ADD) and attention deficit hyperactivity disorder (ADHD).

neurotransmitters Chemicals that carry nerve impulses through the brain.

peer pressure When friends try to convince you to do something you do not want to do in order to conform.

physical addiction When your body cannot function well without a drug.

prescription A written order from a doctor for a medication and instructions for its use.

psychological addiction When your mind craves the high of a drug.

Ritalin The brand name of a prescription drug used to treat attention deficit disorder (ADD) and attention deficit hyperactivity disorder (ADHD).

seizure Potentially fatal convulsions, muscle contractions, and spasms, including those of the heart and brain.

side effect A usually unintended and painful or harmful effect of a drug.

SR Ritalin A long-lasting form of Ritalin.

stimulant A drug that speeds up your brain and body.

street drug An illegally acquired drug.

tolerance When you need more of a drug to get the same effect that you once got from smaller amounts.

withdrawal Painful physical or psychological symptom(s) an addict experiences when he or she stops using drugs.

Where to Go for Help

ORGANIZATIONS

Center for Substance Abuse
Treatment Hotline
(800) 662-4357

Children and Adults with Attention-Deficit/
    Hyperactivity Disorders (CHADD)
8181 Professional Place, Suite 201
Landover, MD 20785
(800) 233-4050
Web site: http://www.chadd.org

Children and Adults with Attention Deficit Disorder
    (CHADD) Vancouver Chapter
P.O. Box 74670
Vancouver BC V6K 4P4
Canada
(604) 222-4043
Web site: http://www.vcn.bc.ca/chaddvan/home.htm

Narcotics Anonymous (NA)
World Services Office
P.O. Box 9999
Van Nuys, CA 91409
(818) 773-9999
(416) 691-9519 (Canada)
e-mail: wso@aol.com
Web site: http://www.na.org

National Center for Learning Disabilities
381 Park Avenue South, Suite 1401
New York, NY 10016
(888) 575-7373
Web site: http://www.ncld.org

PREVLINE: National Clearinghouse for Alcohol
    and Drug Information (NCADI)
P.O. Box 2345
Rockville, MD 20847
(800) 729-6686
e-mail: info@prevline.health.org
Web site: http://www.health.org

The Substance Abuse and Mental Health Service
    Association (SAMHSA)
5600 Fishers Lane
Rockwall II Building, Suite 900
Rockville, MD 20857
(301) 443-0365
e-mail: nnadal@samhsa.gov
Web site: http://www.samhsa.gov

Youth Crisis Hotline
(800) 448-4663

WEB SITES

Due to the changing nature of Internet links, the
Rosen Publishing Group, Inc., has developed an
online list of Web sites related to the subject of this
book. This site is updated regularly. Please use this
link to access the list:

http://www.rosenlinks.com/dpl/rita/

For Further Reading

Beal, Eileen. *Everything You Need to Know About ADD/ADHD*. New York: The Rosen Publishing Group, Inc., 1998.

Clayton, Lawrence. *Amphetamines and Other Stimulants*. Rev. ed. New York: The Rosen Publishing Group, Inc., 1998.

Colvin, Rod. *Prescription Drug Abuse: The Hidden Epidemic*. Omaha, NE: Addicus Books, 1995.

Grosshandler, Janet. *Drugs and the Law*. Rev. ed. New York: The Rosen Publishing Group, Inc., 1997.

Hurwitz, Sue, and Nancy Shniderman. *Drugs and Your Friends*. Rev. ed. New York: The Rosen Publishing Group, Inc. 1995.

Quinn, Patricia. *Adolescents and ADD: Gaining the Advantage*. New York: Magination Press, 1995.

Yoslow, Mark. *Drugs in the Body: Effects of Abuse*. New York: Franklin Watts, 1992.

Index

ABOUT THE AUTHOR

Eileen Beal has an M.A. in history and museum education. She has worked as a junior and senior high-school social studies teacher, an assistant editor for magazines and newspapers, a freelance food and restaurant critic, and a freelance writer. She is a member of the American Medical Writers Association (AMWA). She is also the author of *Choosing a Career in the Restaurant Industry* and *Everything You Need to Know About ADD/ADHD*, both published by the Rosen Publishing Group, Inc.

PHOTO CREDITS

Cover by Christine Innamorato; pp. 2, 14, 35, 42, 48, 53 by Maura B. McConnell; pp. 8, 18, 25, 29, 33 © Daniel T. Brody; p. 21 © Jim Cummins.

SERIES DESIGN

Jordan Zweifler

LAYOUT

Tahara Hasan